I0008939

THE TECH

ENTREPRENEUR'S

POCKET

GUIDE

**Transforming Your Startup Idea into Reality
with Effective Developer Communication**

Dwayne Elahie

THE TECH ENTREPRENEUR'S POCKET GUIDE

Transforming Your Startup Idea into Reality with Effective Developer Communication

Copyright © 2024 by Dwayne Elahie. All rights reserved. No part of this publication may be reproduced, distributed, or transmitted in any form or by any means, including photocopying, recording, or other electronic or mechanical methods, without the prior written permission of the publisher, except in the case of brief quotations embodied in critical reviews and certain other noncommercial uses permitted by copyright law.

ProAnywhere.com

ISBN: 978-1-0688228-0-3

Disclaimer: The author makes no guarantees concerning the level of success you may experience by following the advice and strategies contained in this book, and you accept the risk that results will differ for each individual. The testimonials and examples provided in this book show exceptional results, which may not apply to the average reader, and are not intended to represent or guarantee that anyone will achieve the same or similar results.

"Complexity is just compounded simplicity"

—*Dwayne Elahie*

CONTENTS

PART 1: HOW IT BEGAN

On my first day in a university coding class, I stood alone as the only one without any prior coding experience. As the weeks unfolded, my confusion only deepened; the lectures felt like an alien language, and my pleas for clarity were met with dismissive responses from both the professor and teaching assistants. They suggested that if I couldn't grasp the concepts as quickly as my classmates, perhaps this field wasn't for me. Despite starting my assignments immediately and utilizing every resource available—internet searches, friends' explanations, and the textbook—I managed to pass the class by simply meeting the rubric's criteria, yet without truly understanding a single concept.

The real turning point came after the class concluded. Despite earning an A, I felt it was meaningless if I couldn't apply the knowledge practically, such as developing a video game. This realization led me on a quest for true comprehension. I stumbled upon a coding tutorial series aptly named "talk to me like a 3-year-old," which, through detailed comments rather than traditional tutorials, unravels the mysteries of coding by explaining the intuition behind each line of code. This method illuminated the subject for me, proving that coding could be accessible and understandable. Inspired by Albert Einstein's principle that if you can't explain something simply, you don't understand it well enough, I embarked on a mission to demystify coding for others, starting with teaching children. This approach not only solidified my understanding but also highlighted the flawed notion within prestigious educational systems that only those who can immediately "swim" in the deep end are deemed worthy.

PART 1: HOW IT BEGAN

Years later, I've carried Einstein's wisdom into my professional career, realizing the significant need for clarity in communication between technical and non-technical realms. My ability to simplify complex concepts has been instrumental in my journey, from launching a successful AI startup to leading innovation teams at two Fortune 500 companies. By focusing on clear and accessible communication, I've bridged the gap between business and technical needs, demonstrating that the true mark of understanding is the ability to explain complex ideas in simple terms. This approach has not only advanced my career but has also fostered a more inclusive and supportive environment for innovation and collaboration.

PART 1: HOW IT BEGAN

My name is Dwayne Elahie, and I believe that anyone can learn the fundamentals of creating a tech startup or running a tech project without being thrown into the deep end. By providing them with a guide on what to expect beforehand and helping them understand how things work, we can make the process much smoother.

I'm so grateful for my entrepreneurial experience and fortunate enough to have clients that seek my consultation to help guide them through their journey. That's why I decided to write this guide, so my clients can get a summarized version of what I've learned and experienced over the years, in order for them to better navigate and communicate in the world of tech startups. This is the exact same information I give to all my clients, ensuring we are all on the same page.

I purposefully made this guide short enough to be read in one sitting, aiming to provide the essential information needed for making more strategic decisions early in your endeavor. The alternatives include trying to make it happen on your own without any framework or guidance; or going through a very demanding incubator or accelerator. Such programs can consume 6 to 12 months of your time, require your full-time attention—meaning you must quit your job and possibly neglect relationships—all to learn these same concepts. Additionally, they push you constantly out of your comfort zone to complete tasks by very strict deadlines, and failing to meet these deadlines could result in being expelled from the program.

Don't get me wrong—if you can get into an incubator or accelerator and survive it, you will undoubtedly gain the skills needed to run any startup or tech project. However, if you need this information RIGHT NOW because you are currently starting or are in the middle of your venture, this guide is designed to help you.

Before you dive into this guide, I want to share excerpts from video testimonials of people I have worked with. This is to provide you with the inspiration you need not only to read this guide but also to take it seriously.

Dwayne's method of problem-solving and project scoping ensures technical execution aligns with the business's needs and goals, making projects viable and successful.

—Jermaine Murray, JupiterHR.ca

What Dwayne's really gifted at is turning knowledge into a community thing... He wants to engage with people, he wants people to learn, and none of that surprises me whatsoever.

—Kwesi Davis, Walt Disney Animation Studios

You know, in terms of delivery, we've managed a tour de force—I can say that confidently—by finishing the asset within just eight weeks of work. And it's of ILM quality level. For a normal studio, those kinds of assets could take anywhere from 20 to 50 months; it's crazy, it can take up to a year to complete. But that's precisely why Dwayne and I, along with the team, are so effective. We're extremely flexible, we listen to each other, and we communicate as much as possible.

—Steve Jubinville, DigitalModelCreative.com

Dwayne was great at taking an abstract idea or something where maybe not the most technically sound note that you're receiving from an art director and quickly turn around and sort of organically update the coding, or update the tool to be able to achieve that.

—Chris Ghio, Electronic Arts (EA)

Watch the full video testimonials
https://www.proanywhere.com/testimonials

My hope is that this guide will help you feel confident taking on a new venture and not feel lost like I did in my first programming class.

Enjoy!

PART 2: WHAT I'VE LEARNED

How I Would Build a Startup Now

What I've Learned From My Mistakes

Imagine setting the foundations of a skyscraper. You wouldn't start with the windows or the elevator system; you begin with the core, the base that holds everything together. Similarly, when building a startup, where should your focus lie from the get-go?

Think about a gardener who dreams of a lush, thriving garden. They don't simply scatter seeds randomly; they start by understanding the soil, the garden's specific needs, and what plants will flourish there. Only after this careful preparation do they plant the seeds, ensuring each one has the best chance to grow. This approach isn't just for gardening but is a metaphor for building a successful business. It's about nurturing the right conditions and understanding the ecosystem before you even plant your first seed.

"Start with the customer, not the product. Understand their needs deeply, then build around that knowledge."

✗ **How people intuitively build a business (NOT RECOMMENDED)**
- Find a problem
- Validate that problem
- Build a product to be the solution for that problem
- Build a customer base around the problem

✓ **How I suggest you should build a business**
1. Build a customer base around the problem
2. Find the problem
3. Validate that problem
4. Build a product for that problem

How to build a customer base around the problem
1. **Customer Discovery**: Engage with potential customers to understand their needs and problems.
2. **Customer Validation:** Confirm that the identified problem is real and worth solving.
3. **Customer Creation:** Develop a compelling offer that resonates deeply with your target audience.
   a. **WARNING:** IF YOU DO NOT HAVE THIS, DO NOT MOVE FORWARD BUILDING A COMPANY OR PRODUCT! GO BACK TO CUSTOMER DISCOVERY AND REPEAT THE PROCESS UNTIL YOU HAVE THIS DIALED IN.
4. **Company Building:** Proceed with developing your solution and formalizing your business around the validated problem.

Consider marketing and sales from the beginning:
- **Marketing**: About creating awareness, delivering value, and building customer engagement and loyalty.
- **Sales**: Focuses on converting leads into customers through direct interaction and persuasion.

Marketing sets the stage for sales, making the process smoother and more effective.

The marketing funnel:
- **Awareness:** Introducing your brand to new eyes.
- **Consideration:** Nurturing interested leads with more information.
- **Conversion:** Sealing the deal with a purchase.

I recommend starting by identifying and validating your offer. Begin with one of three strategies: pre-selling your product or service, conducting a paid pilot, or securing letters of intent (LOI) based on your offer. If there's no interest, it's crucial to reassess your offer. Often, startups pivot because their initial proposition didn't connect with their audience, prompting the need for a more compelling offer.

Pre-selling your product or service based solely on the concept itself serves as a strong indicator of your target audience's genuine interest. A common hesitation I hear is, 'I can't sell a product that hasn't been created yet.' My counterargument is drawn from the entertainment industry, which routinely pre-sells movies through trailers, sparking excitement and securing sales well before the final product is available.

Another viable approach involves conducting a paid pilot, ideally priced between $5,000 and $10,000. While this investment may seem significant for an individual, it is relatively modest for a company. This level of financial commitment, typically requiring an approval process, signifies traction and hints at a potential demand for your offering.

However, a letter of intent (LOI), being a non-binding agreement where a prospect expresses an intention to buy your product or service at a predetermined price once available, ranks as the least effective method to demonstrate traction or demand. It is, nonetheless, preferable to having no validation at all.

Continuous iteration of your product or service is crucial. This involves regularly soliciting feedback from your customers and making significant enhancements based on their insights. The entertainment industry exemplifies this through the use of storyboards in film production. Storyboards, basic visual representations of scenes, serve as the minimal viable product (MVP) and undergo validation by a test audience. This feedback informs continuous refinements to the script and storyboards. This iterative process repeats until a version emerges that resonates well with the majority of the target audience, or until the timeline necessitates a decision on whether to proceed with full-scale production.

I suggest applying this iterative, feedback-driven approach to your startup's products and services. By adopting a strategy akin to the film industry's storyboard process, you can more effectively validate and refine your offering to meet your target audience's needs and preferences.

Imagine a startup that begins by deeply engaging with its potential market, identifying a core problem many face yet haven't found a solution for. They conduct thorough customer discovery, refining their understanding and ensuring they validate the need. Only then do they begin to shape their offer, all while laying the groundwork for their marketing and sales strategies. By the time they're ready to introduce their product, they have a ready and waiting customer base, aware of the brand and eager for a solution.

"To build a startup that stands the test of time, begin with your customer's needs. Let their problems guide your product development, and let your early focus on marketing and sales light the path to success."

Deciding to Build Your Startup

Is Starting a Startup Right for You?

Why every aspiring entrepreneur should embrace resilience as their guiding star.

Consider the Japanese art of Kintsugi, where broken pottery is mended with gold, silver, or platinum, highlighting the beauty in imperfection and resilience. This philosophy teaches that objects, much like humans, gain more value and uniqueness through overcoming adversity. It's a powerful metaphor for life, illustrating that the challenges and failures we face are not just obstacles but opportunities to become stronger, more unique, and more valuable.

The principle is... Resilience transforms challenges into the gold of personal and professional growth.

In the realm of startups, I once encountered a founder who embodied the essence of resilience. This individual launched a venture that, despite initial enthusiasm, faced numerous setbacks. User acquisition was sluggish, funding was hard to come by, and the roadmap to success seemed ever-elusive. Instead of succumbing to despair, the founder viewed each setback as a lesson, iterating on the product, refining the pitch to investors, and deepening the understanding of the market. With persistence, the company gradually gained traction, transforming from a struggling startup to a market leader. This journey wasn't just about building a successful business; it was a testament to the founder's resilience, turning potential failures into stepping stones towards success.

Remember, resilience is not just about enduring hardships; it's about using them as a forge for personal and professional development. It's the golden glue that binds and strengthens, transforming challenges into victories.

The Upside of Leaving Your FAANG Position

Why making the leap from a FAANG job could be your most liberating career move.

Consider the traditional path many seek for security: climbing the corporate ladder at a prestigious company, acquiring wealth and status. This journey is akin to a ship sailing in familiar waters, its course charted by countless others. The allure of the unknown seas, however, calls to the adventurous spirit, promising discovery and the chance to chart one's own path. The FAANG companies (Facebook, Apple, Amazon, Netflix, Google) represent the pinnacle of the familiar path, offering security, prestige, and comfort. Yet, the call of the entrepreneurial spirit beckons some to venture into uncharted waters, despite the allure of the known.

The principle is... The true essence of adventure and personal fulfillment lies in navigating the uncharted, not anchoring in the harbor of comfort.

Many tech talents at FAANG companies dream of starting their own ventures, of breaking free from golden handcuffs. These handcuffs are not just financial incentives but psychological traps: the promise of upward mobility, the seduction of working on 'moonshot' projects, and the gradual upscaling of lifestyle that makes leaving financially difficult. Yet, those who dare to leave often find that the skills and habits acquired at FAANG, while valuable, don't directly translate to the startup world. The true journey of an entrepreneur begins with unlearning, with shedding the security blanket of corporate life to embrace the uncertainty and freedom of building something from scratch. This journey, while fraught with challenges, is rich in learning and personal growth, offering rewards no corporate job can match.

Remember, the call to venture beyond the comfortable and familiar, to explore the unknown, is where true growth and fulfillment lie. It's not the safety of the known but the thrill of the adventure that shapes us, urging us to leave the FAANG harbor and sail into entrepreneurial seas.

Why You Should Consider Starting a Startup

Why the journey from joining a startup to possibly creating your own is a path worth considering, despite uncertainties and potential failures.

In the medieval era, venturing beyond one's village to explore or settle in new lands was deemed perilous and foolish, akin to today's fear of leaving a stable job to start a venture. Yet, those who dared to explore often discovered new opportunities and horizons, changing the course of their lives and, sometimes, history. This spirit of exploration and the willingness to embrace the unknown for the chance of achieving something greater is a timeless narrative that resonates across generations, mirroring the journey of a startup founder.

The principle is... Embracing uncertainty and the willingness to fail is the bedrock of transformative success.

Consider the early days of Y Combinator, a pioneer in startup acceleration, which bet on the potential of young founders right out of college, some as young as 19. Despite prevailing beliefs about the necessity of experience, age, or even a concrete business plan, these founders were encouraged to dive into the startup world. This leap of faith, grounded in the belief that determination and the ability to learn from failures are more crucial than initial success, led to the creation of groundbreaking companies and, for many, personal fortunes that exceeded their dreams. This journey from uncertainty to success underscores the value of perseverance, a willingness to learn, and the courage to embrace failure as a stepping stone to innovation.

Remember, the path less trodden, filled with uncertainties and potential failures, often leads to the most significant breakthroughs and personal growth. It's not the fear of failure but the courage to confront it and persist that defines true success.

Laying the Groundwork for Your Startup Journey

Why the leap into founding a startup requires a shift from conventional wisdom to embracing the counterintuitive.

Imagine a young musician learning to play the violin. Initially, her instincts tell her to grip the bow tightly for control. However, her teacher advises a counterintuitive approach: hold the bow lightly to allow for fluid movement and finer control. This adjustment feels unnatural at first, but as she practices, this new way becomes second nature, leading to a more expressive and masterful performance. This journey mirrors the startup experience, where initial instincts often lead astray, and success comes from learning, sometimes counterintuitively, what truly resonates with your audience.

The principle is... Success in startups, as in music, comes from mastering the counterintuitive, learning to play by a different set of rules.

In the world of startups, this principle manifests in the founders' journey from idea to execution. Founders often begin with a set of assumptions about what success looks like — chasing funding, scaling quickly, or following the latest trend. However, those who find true success do so by focusing deeply on understanding their users' needs, often discovering that these needs are far removed from their initial assumptions. This focus on the user, even when it leads away from the conventional startup playbook, is what allows them to create products that resonate deeply and stand the test of time.

Remember, the path to startup success is paved with lessons that often run counter to our initial instincts. Embrace the

counterintuitive, focus on learning deeply about what matters —
your users — and let that knowledge guide you to solutions that
truly resonate.

The Startup Idea Lifecycle: From Conception to Validation

Nurturing and Testing Ideas for Startup Success

Imagine standing at the crossroads of creation, where every
path seems to lead to the unknown. This is the beginning of
your journey into the startup world. The first step isn't finding the
path everyone else is taking but spotting the one that's uniquely
yours.

Consider the story of the Wright brothers. They didn't invent the concept of flight; they observed, experimented, and iterated on the ideas that came before them, driven by a deep, personal passion for solving the problem of human flight. Their success wasn't predetermined; it was their unique approach, perspective, and relentless pursuit that made all the difference.

"Fall in love with the problem, not the solution." Your mission isn't to invent a desire but to find a genuine need and fulfill it.

Reflect on the founders of a small startup, who noticed how fragmented and inefficient the process of getting reliable construction supplies was. They weren't industry giants or had groundbreaking tech; they simply listened to a common frustration they had experienced themselves and sought to make it better. Their solution became indispensable to their users because it addressed a real, tangible need.

Remember, the most groundbreaking innovations often come from looking at ordinary problems through a lens of genuine curiosity and a desire to make things better. So, when seeking the seed of your next venture, look around you. The problems you encounter every day, no matter how mundane they may seem, could be the birthplace of your next great idea.

The Entrepreneur's Illusion: Tempting Ideas That Fail

Why some startup ideas seem irresistible but lead to failure.

Imagine stumbling upon what looks like a freshwater pond in a vast desert, a rare and tempting sight. This is akin to discovering a startup idea that appears unique and unexplored, promising an easy path to success because no one else seems to be drinking from this pond. You're excited, thinking you've found an untapped opportunity. However, this pond is actually a tar pit, sticky and deceptive. It looks inviting, but once you step in, you find yourself stuck, unable to move forward or escape, while the reality of its danger slowly sinks in. This is a common trap many founders fall into with certain startup ideas.

Beware the allure of tar pit ideas; they're seductive but perilous.

The founders of numerous startups have been lured by the appeal of tar pit ideas, such as creating an app for discovering new things or betting software. These ideas seem promising due to their apparent novelty and lack of competition. However, upon diving in, founders often find themselves unable to make progress, stuck in a market with no demand or overshadowed by unforeseen complexities. They ignore signs of danger, seduced by the pond's deceptive tranquility, until they find themselves too deep to easily pivot away.

The most enticing startup ideas can sometimes be the most dangerous. Success lies in recognizing and avoiding these tar pits, instead seeking paths less trodden but with real potential for impact and growth.

Discovering Your Next Big Startup Concept

Ever wonder why so many innovations or startups seem to emerge out of nowhere and change everything? It often starts with someone's personal frustration.

Consider the legend of Archimedes in his bath, suddenly understanding how to measure the volume of an object while he himself was submerged in water. This moment of clarity didn't come from trying to think of a great idea; it came from a personal experience and a problem he encountered in his everyday life. Just like Archimedes, modern innovators often stumble upon their greatest ideas not by searching for something to invent, but by living their lives and paying attention to the problems they face.

Great innovations are often personal solutions in disguise.

A group of friends, frustrated by their inability to share expenses easily on trips, decided to build a simple app to solve their problem. Initially, it was just for personal use, but soon they realized many others faced the same issue. This app, born out of personal need, grew into a widely used financial tool, transforming the way people manage shared expenses.

Remember, the most impactful innovations often come from solving problems you intimately understand. Keep your eyes open for everyday inconveniences; your solution to a personal problem might just be the next big thing.

Pivot to Prosper: Transforming Challenges into Opportunities

Embarking on the entrepreneurial journey is akin to setting sail on uncharted waters. It's thrilling, fraught with unknowns, and often, calls for a change in direction. Understanding when and how to pivot your startup idea is not just strategic—it's survival.

Consider the story of an ancient mariner navigating by the stars. Amidst their voyage, they encounter unpredictable storms and shifting winds, demanding immediate course corrections. These adjustments, though small and often based on gut feelings, are critical for reaching their destination. Similarly, startups face turbulent markets and unforeseen challenges that necessitate a pivot, a strategic shift in business model, product, or target audience to stay afloat and thrive.

The principle is..."Success in startups is about steering, not just speed. It's the wise pivots that lead to legendary journeys."

A tech startup begins by developing a novel social media platform, only to discover that engagement is low, and growth is stagnant despite months of effort. Refusing to be disheartened, the team leverages their technology to pivot towards a more niche, yet highly engaged market—professional networking for artists. This pivot, fueled by direct feedback and a deep understanding of a specific user's pain points, turns their initial struggle into a thriving platform.

In the dynamic landscape of startups, adaptability and responsiveness to feedback are your greatest assets. Remember, it's the well-timed pivots, informed by insight and courage, that can transform an uncertain voyage into a legendary expedition. Embrace the pivot as not just a strategy, but a mindset of continuous evolution towards success.

Against the Grain: How Contrarian Ideas Fuel Startup Success

Why brilliant ideas often appear foolish at first glance.

Consider the story of a group of inventors who embarked on creating the first airplane. At their time, the consensus was that human flight was an impossibility, a notion reserved for the birds and the domain of fantasy. Yet, these inventors saw beyond the limitations of the present, driven by a vision of a world transformed by the ability to soar through the skies. Their relentless pursuit, in the face of skepticism and ridicule, was fueled by a deep understanding of the principles of aerodynamics they discovered through direct experience and experimentation, not by accepting the prevailing wisdom of their day.

The principle is... True innovation often comes from contrarian thinking, not consensus.

This mirrors the journey of startup founders who launched platforms that transformed the way we live, work, and connect. These founders faced criticism and disbelief because they dared to challenge the status quo and solve problems in a way that seemed unfeasible to most. They didn't just imagine a new solution; they experienced the very problems they aimed to solve. By using their firsthand experiences as a compass, they navigated through the sea of skepticism to create solutions that were initially dismissed as folly but later became indispensable.

Remember, true innovation often comes from contrarian thinking, not consensus. It's the courage to pursue what others deem impossible that leads to groundbreaking discoveries and the creation of new worlds of possibility.

Structuring Your Founding Team

Essential Elements of Co-Founder Synergy

Why embarking on a startup journey solo might feel heroic but often leads to uncharted territories of challenges.

Imagine the Wright brothers attempting their first flight. While they both had unique strengths, it was their combined efforts, mutual support, and shared vision that eventually led to the historic moment at Kitty Hawk. Their partnership exemplifies the power of collaboration, where two minds, when united, can achieve what seems impossible alone.

Unity in vision and diversity in skills fortifies the foundation of groundbreaking achievements.

In the world of startups, there's a tale of two co-founders who met through a co-founder matching platform. One brought a groundbreaking idea and relentless passion, while the other contributed technical genius and a meticulous approach to problem-solving. Initially, they encountered skepticism – the market was crowded, and their idea seemed like a long shot. Yet, by leveraging their combined strengths, embracing each other's perspectives, and dividing roles based on their unique expertise, they transformed their concept into a revolutionary product. Their startup didn't just survive; it thrived, securing significant funding and making a notable impact in their industry.

Remember, the synergy of a well-aligned co-founder partnership transcends the sum of its parts, turning visionary ideas into tangible successes.

Avoiding the Co-Founder Traps That Doom Startups

Launching a venture with a co-founder can significantly amplify your success, akin to having a superpower by your side. Yet, embarking on this journey unprepared can spell disaster.

Imagine two friends embarking on a cross-country road trip. Initially, the excitement masks their lack of planning. However, as challenges arise—flat tires, disagreements over directions, diverging interests in pit stops—their journey becomes strained. The situation worsens because they never discussed how to handle disagreements or distribute responsibilities. Eventually, what was meant to be an epic adventure turns into a silent drive, with each wishing they had journeyed alone. This could have been avoided if they had set clear expectations, agreed on a decision-making process, and embraced the significance of their partnership from the start.

The foundation of any successful partnership, be it in business or life, lies in clear communication, mutual respect, and predefined resolutions for conflicts.

In the startup world, two entrepreneurs decide to bring their innovative idea to life. Inspired by the principle of clear communication, they spend time discussing not just their business vision but also how they will address disagreements, share responsibilities, and support each other through stress. They agree on a fair equity split and define roles that leverage their strengths. When challenges arise, as they inevitably do, this groundwork allows them to navigate disagreements constructively, leading to a stronger bond and a thriving business. Their startup doesn't just survive; it flourishes because its foundation is built on trust and mutual respect.

To ensure your venture's success, prioritize establishing a strong, transparent partnership with your co-founder. This involves clear communication, fair agreements, and a shared commitment to overcome obstacles together. By doing so, you transform potential pitfalls into opportunities for growth, reinforcing the principle that the right partnership is indeed a superpower in the entrepreneurial journey.

Dividing the Dream: How to Fairly Split Equity Among Founders

Deciding how to distribute equity among co-founders is more than just a negotiation; it's a strategic move to ensure the long-term success and motivation of your team.

Imagine two startups, both with brilliant ideas and passionate teams. Startup A decides on equity distribution through tough negotiations, focusing on immediate contributions. Startup B considers long-term motivation, granting equity that reflects not just the present input but the anticipated hard work and dedication over the years. Fast forward four years, Startup A struggles with motivation and co-founder disputes, while Startup B thrives, with co-founders driven by a strong sense of ownership and commitment to their shared vision.

Equity isn't just about value now, it's about motivating commitment for the marathon ahead.

A CEO of a rising tech startup faced early co-founder disagreements. Instead of sticking rigidly to initial equity allocations based on current inputs, they revisited the equity split, considering long-term roles and potential contributions. Implementing four-year vesting with a one-year cliff ensured commitment, while the more generous equity strategy fostered a deeply motivated and cohesive team, driving the startup through tough times to remarkable success.

Remember, fair and strategic equity splits among co-founders are crucial not just for recognizing present contributions, but more importantly, for securing and motivating the team's long-term dedication and success.

Building Strong Working Relationships

Imagine a team working together harmoniously, their synergy is undeniable. Yet, when disagreements arise, as they inevitably will, their ability to navigate these challenges determines their success. It's not the absence of conflict that defines a successful partnership, but how that conflict is managed.

Consider the insights of John Gottman, who studied marriages to predict their success based on how couples handle disagreements. Gottman found that it's not the avoidance of fights that matters but the methods used to resolve them. Every partnership, whether in marriage or business, will face similar disputes over resources, priorities, or decisions.

The principle here is clear: "It's not the fights that matter, but how we fight." This echoes in every type of close relationship, including those among co-founders. The way disagreements are handled can either strengthen the bond or lead to a partnership's downfall.

In a startup environment, founders can apply this principle by establishing clear roles, understanding each other's attachment styles, documenting processes for handling disagreements, and practicing nonviolent communication. These strategies not only prevent the escalation of conflict but also ensure that all members feel heard and valued, fostering a culture of mutual respect and understanding.

Remember, the key to enduring partnerships isn't avoiding conflict but embracing a constructive approach to resolving disagreements. "It's not the fights that matter, but how we fight." This mindset will pave the way for more resilient and successful collaborations.

Building Blocks of a Minimum Viable Product (MVP)

Building Better Products by Talking to Your Users

Imagine you're embarking on a journey to create something incredible, a product or service that could change lives. But where do you start? The foundation of any successful endeavor lies in understanding those you're aiming to serve.

Picture the early days of the most influential companies we know today. Their founders didn't just sit in isolation, crafting products based on what they thought people needed. Instead, they reached out, engaged in conversations, and most importantly, listened. They understood that the secret sauce to their future success was learning directly from their potential users or customers.

The principle is simple - your users hold the key to your success. Engaging with them from the outset is not just beneficial; it's crucial. They provide the insights and feedback necessary to shape your product into something that not only meets needs but exceeds expectations.

Start by identifying and reaching out to potential users. Use platforms like LinkedIn, forums, or community events to find those who might benefit from what you're creating. Then, engage in genuine conversations with them. Ask open-ended questions to understand their challenges and needs deeply. Avoid leading questions that could bias their responses. Throughout this process, listen more than you speak, and resist the urge to sell your idea. Instead, focus on absorbing their insights.

Remember, the principle at the heart of this journey is that direct engagement with your users is the cornerstone of building something truly impactful. By understanding their needs, challenges, and desires, you're not just building a product; you're solving real problems.

Effectively Communicating With Dev Team

Imagine standing at the helm of a ship, navigating through the complex waters of software development. The journey from concept to completion is fraught with challenges, yet understanding the language of your crew, charting the course, and steering the ship with precision can lead to uncharted territories of innovation and success.

Consider the construction of a towering skyscraper. Before the first steel beam is erected, architects and builders spend countless hours ensuring they speak the same language, visualizing the end structure, and meticulously planning each step. This harmonious collaboration between vision and execution is akin to the dance between a development team and project management, ensuring the project's foundation is as strong as the communication that supports it.

Building software is an art and science, where clear communication, shared vision, and precise tracking turn ideas into digital realities.

Step 1 - Establish a Common Language:

- Demystify coding concepts to foster:
  - A deep understanding of coding language and its application.
  - Enhanced communication leading to seamless collaboration.
- Achievements:
  - Cultivate a unified environment where ideas flow freely.
  - Ensure project objectives are crystal clear to everyone involved.

Step 2 - Visualize the User Journey:

- Reverse-engineer the process by:
  - Starting with the end goal and working backward.
  - Prioritizing the desired outcome from the outset.
- Achievements:
  - Pinpoint potential hurdles and areas ripe for enhancement.
  - Forge a pathway that aligns technical prowess with business strategy, eliminating miscommunication with the tech team.

Step 3 - Track and Monitor the Project:

- Key actions include:
    - Setting clear business goals, KPIs, and objectives.
    - Employing effective management methodologies tailored to the team's makeup.
- Achievements:
    - Cultivate a cohesive, motivated, and efficient project team.
    - Derive actionable insights to guide future decisions.
    - Position yourself as a pivotal figure in the project's success, ready to offer informed recommendations.

Envision a scenario where you, as the project lead, embark on a new software development project. Initially, the gap between your vision and the development team's understanding seems wide. However, by establishing a common language, you start seeing eye to eye, discussing complex coding paradigms as if they were no more complicated than a daily grocery list. Next, by visualizing the user journey together, you align every line of code with the user's needs and business objectives, ensuring every team member not only sees but feels the direction and purpose. Finally, with meticulous tracking and regular insights analysis, your project not only meets but exceeds expectations, solidifying your status as a visionary leader.

Effectively communicating with your development team is the cornerstone of turning visionary ideas into functional software. By establishing a common language, visualizing the user journey, and tracking progress with precision, you elevate your project from concept to creation, ensuring success at every turn.

Do you want to be able to understand coding,

- In the next 30 days
- That only takes as little as 30 minutes of practice a day
- that is simple enough for anyone to learn
- So you will be 30 to 40 times more effective in communicating with your development team

And WITHOUT you having to do an intensive coding bootcamp or go back to school to get a degree to become a developer yourself?

Our program provides immersive training in effective communication strategies, code literacy, and project management essentials, enabling you to seamlessly bridge the gap between your vision and your development team's execution.

You can check out the details at ProAnywhere.com/coding

Quick to Market: Strategies for Building Your MVP

Why starting with a minimum viable product (MVP) is your quickest path to success.

Consider the story of the humble bamboo plant. It spends its initial years growing roots, barely visible above the surface. This phase doesn't show much progress to the outside world, yet it's crucial for what comes next. Then, in a matter of weeks, it shoots up to towering heights. This growth spurt is possible only because of the strong foundation laid during those initial, seemingly unproductive years.

"Great oaks from little acorns grow" – Every colossal achievement begins with a simple, small step.

Think about the origins of now-giant companies like Airbnb and Twitch. Airbnb started without a payment system, relying on in-person cash exchanges. Twitch, originally Justin.tv, began as a single-channel live-streaming platform with no gaming content. Both were far from perfect, embodying the MVP concept by starting simple and building from there based on user feedback and iteration. Despite their humble beginnings, they laid the groundwork for monumental success.

Remember, every grand achievement begins with a simple step. Start with an MVP, embrace feedback, iterate, and don't get too attached to the initial version. Your MVP is merely the first step on your journey to greatness.

Building a Product from Idea to Launch: Fundamental Steps

Imagine starting a journey with a simple map, sketching your path with broad strokes. You're on a quest not just for treasure, but for knowledge and growth.

Think back to the explorers of old, setting sail into the unknown with just a compass and the stars to guide them. Their voyages weren't about reaching a destination quickly; they were about discovery, learning from the sea, the weather, and the lands they encountered. Each journey was a cycle of planning, setting out, facing challenges, adapting, and then returning home richer not just in gold, but in invaluable experiences.

The journey is as valuable as the destination.

In the realm of building something groundbreaking, like a new app or product, the cycle is strikingly similar. Consider a team embarking on developing a new software tool. They started with a clear cycle, set goals like increasing user engagement, and held brainstorming sessions where all ideas were welcome. By organizing these ideas into categories, they could prioritize and decide collectively. Through concise specifications and defined success metrics, each team member knew their role. This process wasn't about launching the perfect product instantly but about evolving through continuous, measured steps. Their journey of development, testing, and iteration mirrored the explorers of the past—navigating through the unknown, learning, and adapting.

Just as explorers valued the journey for its lessons and discoveries, successful product development is about valuing each cycle of creation, feedback, and improvement. The journey is as valuable as the destination.

Product Launch

The Cycle of Success: Launch, Learn, Relaunch

Imagine embarking on a journey to build a boat. You've envisioned a sleek, powerful vessel that glides effortlessly through the water. Yet, the first version you construct might barely float, let alone sail. This scenario isn't a failure but a crucial step in the process.

Consider the story of a renowned sculptor who begins with a rough block of marble. With each chisel strike, the artist removes pieces of the stone, gradually revealing the masterpiece within. The first strike isn't meant to be perfect—it's a necessary action that leads to refinement and, eventually, to the creation of a stunning sculpture. This process of continuous improvement is vital, not just in art, but in every endeavor we pursue, especially in launching startups.

Perfection is achieved not when there's nothing more to add, but when there's nothing left to take away. This principle teaches us that true excellence comes from refinement and iteration, not from getting it right on the first try.

In the world of startups, this principle is epitomized by the journey of Airbnb. They didn't find immediate success; in fact, they launched three times before gaining traction. Each launch was a learning opportunity, allowing them to understand their users better, refine their product, and adjust their approach. This persistence and willingness to iterate transformed Airbnb from a barely floating idea into a powerful vessel that changed the way we travel.

Remember, the path to excellence is a journey of continuous improvement. Whether you're sculpting marble, building a boat, or launching a startup, the key is to start, learn, refine, and repeat. It's not about launching perfectly but launching persistently.

First Customer Success: Strategies for New Startups

Transforming the daunting into the doable, let's talk about turning users into your first customers.

Consider the story of a small café that opened in a quiet town. Initially, the café saw very few visitors despite offering excellent coffee. The owner decided to personally invite people from the community to visit, offering a unique experience rather than just a cup of coffee. They listened to feedback, adjusted their offerings, and within months, word of mouth made the café a bustling social hub. This tale illustrates the power of hands-on, personalized efforts in turning a challenging situation around.

"Growth through personal touch" – Success comes from engaging directly and deeply with your first users.

In the early days of a now globally recognized tech company, the founders personally onboarded their first users, meticulously gathered feedback, and refined their product accordingly. This direct interaction not only led to invaluable insights but also built a loyal customer base that felt heard and valued. Their commitment to personal touch in these initial interactions laid the foundation for exponential growth.

Remember, the key to transforming users into loyal customers lies in the principle of "Growth through personal touch." Engage directly, listen carefully, and adapt swiftly.

Growth Beyond Scale: Embracing the Inefficiencies

Imagine starting a journey, not with the roar of engines on a clear, wide road, but with a manual crank on a path less traveled. This beginning might seem modest, yet it's the essence of transforming an idea into a phenomenon.

Consider the story of a village's annual fair, famous for its unique and handcrafted goods. Every year, artisans and crafters from the village and beyond would come to showcase their creations. Among them was a young potter who, instead of mass-producing his pottery on a wheel as many did, chose to sculpt each piece by hand. His process was slow and painstaking, often yielding fewer pieces than his counterparts. However, his dedication to craftsmanship and the unique touch he gave each pot drew a small, but incredibly loyal, following. Over time, this following grew, not because of the quantity of his work, but because of the unparalleled quality and the story behind each piece.

True growth begins with embracing the unscalable.

In the tech world, this principle comes to life through startups. For instance, a new app aimed at connecting local farmers with urban consumers started with the founders personally visiting farms. They selected a few to feature on their platform, ensuring each product met their high standards. This hands-on approach was labor-intensive and seemingly unscalable, yet it established a foundation of trust and quality that automated systems couldn't replicate. As word spread, more farmers wanted to join, and the user base grew organically. The initial unscalable efforts paid off, setting the app apart in a crowded market.

Remember, the journey of a thousand miles begins with a single step, often taken by hand. True growth begins with embracing the unscalable.

Growth and Revenue

Achieving Your Goals: How to Define KPIs and Prioritize Time

Why understanding your startup's true north is critical.

Think about a ship navigating the vast ocean. Without a compass, it's just drifting, susceptible to the whims of the current and wind. The captain knows the destination, but reaching it requires constant adjustments, keen observation, and sometimes, hard choices about what to discard to stay afloat and on course. This journey isn't just about reaching the destination; it's about navigating the challenges intelligently and efficiently, ensuring every action pushes the ship closer to where it needs to be.

Your startup's success hinges on identifying and relentlessly pursuing your 'True North.'

Imagine a startup as a ship, embarking on a voyage towards the coveted island of Product-Market Fit. The seas are unpredictable, filled with competing priorities and endless tasks.

By setting a 'True North'—a clear, overarching goal—this startup can navigate through the turbulent waters. This 'True North' could be as straightforward as 'Revenue Growth.' Each day, the founder acts as the captain, making decisions, big and small, all aimed at steering closer to their goal. They might decide to focus on improving customer experience over adding new features or choose to refine an onboarding process to convert more trial users into paying customers. By always aligning actions with their 'True North,' they ensure that every effort contributes directly to their voyage towards success.

Remember, the journey of a startup is about more than just moving forward; it's about moving in the right direction. Identifying your startup's 'True North'—your primary KPI—and aligning every action towards it, ensures you're not just busy, but productively steering towards your destination of growth and success.

Startup Business Model and Pricing Structure

Why do many startups struggle with business models and pricing, yet a few master the art effortlessly?

Consider the journey of a renowned chef who decides to open a new restaurant. At first, they experiment with various cuisines and menu pricing strategies, trying to find the perfect match that will attract and retain customers. They test different menu items, adjust prices, and monitor customer responses and sales data closely. This process of experimentation, learning from feedback, and continuous adjustment is akin to a startup navigating its business model and pricing strategy.

Success lies in adapting proven frameworks to your unique recipe and continuously refining based on customer feedback.

A tech startup, inspired by the successes of giants in their industry, adopts a SaaS model with a subscription-based pricing strategy. Initially, they set a low price to attract users but soon realize through customer feedback that their users are willing to pay more for the added value and features they provide. Gradually, they increase their prices, improving their product based on user suggestions, and soon they find a sweet spot that maximizes both user growth and revenue.

Remember, the key to mastering your startup's business model and pricing is not to reinvent the wheel but to adapt proven methods to your unique offering and refine them based on customer insights.

Navigating Growth: Strategies for Startups

Discover the universal key to startup success, regardless of your industry or current stage.

Consider a gardener nurturing a variety of plants, each requiring different care - sunlight for some, shade for others, more water here, less there. This gardener knows that to see growth, they must understand each plant's unique needs and adapt their care accordingly. This approach isn't just about gardening; it applies universally to nurturing startups.

Tailored nurturing leads to growth. Understanding and adapting to your startup's unique needs and market conditions is crucial for success.

For a startup, this might mean identifying your core customer base and focusing intensely on serving their specific needs before scaling. Initially, engage in activities that don't necessarily scale, such as personalized outreach or bespoke service offerings, to deeply understand and solve your customers' problems. As the startup matures, shift towards scalable growth tactics and channels, continually testing and adapting strategies based on data-driven insights.

Remember, just like the gardener with their plants, the secret to fostering growth in your startup lies in tailored nurturing - understanding and adapting to your unique circumstances and needs. This approach ensures strong roots and sustainable growth.

The Journey of Fundraising and Company Creation

From Idea to Investment: How Startup Fundraising Works

Unveiling the realities of startup fundraising: It's more accessible than you think.

Imagine two aspiring entrepreneurs, both with groundbreaking ideas. One is caught in the web of myths about fundraising—believing it requires a glamorous pitch, an impressive network, and accepting loss of control. The other sees past these myths, understanding that fundraising is about conviction and leveraging the right tools. The latter embarks on a journey, utilizing simple tools and straightforward conversations, focusing on what truly matters: building something people want.

Fundraising is a bridge, not a barrier, to bringing your vision to life.

Consider a startup that began with a simple version of their product, minimal users, and no formal network. They faced rejections but persisted, focusing on product development and direct dialogues with investors using accessible tools like SAFEs. This approach not only secured them the necessary funds but also preserved their control over the company, allowing them to grow on their terms.

Remember, the essence of successful fundraising isn't in the grandeur of your presentation or the depth of your connections. It lies in your commitment to your idea and your ability to communicate its value straightforwardly. Fundraising is a bridge that, when navigated with clarity and determination, brings you closer to realizing your vision.

The Leader's Journey: From Aspiring to Inspiring

Leadership transcends a singular style, evolving into a unique blend of communication, judgment, and integrity.

Imagine a mosaic, each piece representing a different leadership trait or style. Some pieces are vibrant, catching the eye with their charisma, while others are subtle, their strength lying in quiet determination. Together, these pieces form a complete picture, illustrating that leadership does not conform to one specific pattern. Each leader contributes a distinct piece to the mosaic, their individuality enhancing the overall design. This diversity in leadership styles mirrors the natural world, where a variety of ecosystems thrive, each with its unique harmony.

True leadership flourishes on the foundation of authenticity, nurturing trust through clear communication, sound judgment about people, and unwavering personal integrity.

Consider a leader who embraces their unique attributes, leveraging their genuine self to inspire and guide their team. This leader understands that clarity in communication illuminates the path forward, making complex ideas accessible to all. They exercise discernment in their relationships, recognizing and cultivating the potential in others. Most importantly, they lead with integrity, their actions consistently reflecting their values and mission. This approach fosters a deep-seated trust, empowering their team to achieve collective goals with confidence and commitment.

Embrace your individuality as a leader, for it is your authenticity that will inspire trust and loyalty. By communicating with clarity, exercising sound judgment, and upholding your integrity, you create a legacy of leadership that resonates with truth and effectiveness. Leadership is not about fitting a mold but about being true to yourself and leading with conviction and care.

PART 3: WHAT'S NEXT

If you found value in this guide and would like more, consider joining ProAnywhere.

ProAnywhere

Do you want to be able to understand coding,

- In the next 30 days
- That only takes as little as 30 minutes of practice a day
- that is simple enough for anyone to learn
- So you will be 30 to 40 times more effective in communicating with your development team

And WITHOUT you having to do an intensive coding bootcamp or go back to school to get a degree to become a developer yourself?

Our program provides immersive training in effective communication strategies, code literacy, and project management essentials, enabling you to seamlessly bridge the gap between your vision and your development team's execution.

You can check out the details at ProAnywhere.com/coding

Many will come across our offer, feel a spark of possibility, but ultimately, they'll let that spark fade. That's the path of "most people."

I urge you not to follow in those footsteps. Allow me to share a story that highlights the transformative power of action.

Once, I found myself at a crossroads in my career. I was part of a tech startup that was floundering, with a project so riddled with miscommunication and delays that it seemed doomed to fail. The vision was there, but the bridge between our non-technical leadership and the development team was non-existent. It was a repeating pattern in my career, one that left me feeling like I was always on the brink of something great, only to watch it slip through my fingers.

In a moment of clarity, driven by the fear of watching another project implode, I decided to take a leap. I enrolled in a course designed to enhance communication between project managers and developers. It was a commitment - of time, of resources, of ego. The thought of embracing a completely new approach was daunting. But the alternative? Remaining stuck in a cycle of frustration and missed opportunities.

That decision marked the turning point. The course wasn't just about learning to speak the language of code; it was about reshaping my approach to leadership and collaboration. It empowered me to not only envision the success of our projects but to actively steer them towards that success.

And it worked. Our projects transformed from stagnant to dynamic, from fraught with misunderstanding to characterized by seamless collaboration. It was as if I had discovered a new superpower. The impact on my career was immediate and profound. I wasn't just participating in projects; I was leading them to new heights of success.

Now, it's your chance. This isn't just about acquiring a new skill set; it's about fundamentally changing how you interact with your team and your projects. It's about moving from the sidelines to being a central figure in your project's success.

You have the opportunity to start this journey with us. Visit ProAnywhere.com/coding to explore how our program can transform you from a project participant into a project superstar.

Don't let hesitation hold you back. Take that step, embrace the change, and discover what you're truly capable of. Even if our program isn't the right fit for you, I encourage you to take action in some way, shape, or form. Your future success depends on the actions you take today. All you have to do is BEGIN.

You can check out the details at
ProAnywhere.com/coding

www.ingramcontent.com/pod-product-compliance
Lightning Source LLC
Chambersburg PA
CBHW042024080326
R17960500001B/R179605PG40689CBX00019B/1